BRITAIN IN PICTURES
THE BRITISH PEOPLE IN PICTURES

ENGLISH LETTER WRITERS

GENERAL EDITOR
W. J. TURNER

The Editor is most grateful to all those who have
so kindly helped in the selection of illustrations
especially to officials of the various public
Museums Libraries and Galleries and
to all others who have generously
allowed pictures and MSS
to be reproduced

ENGLISH
LETTER WRITERS

C. E. VULLIAMY

WITH
8 PLATES IN COLOUR
AND
24 ILLUSTRATIONS IN
BLACK & WHITE

COLLINS · 14 ST. JAMES'S PLACE · LONDON
MCMXLVI

PRODUCED BY
ADPRINT LIMITED LONDON

FIRST PUBLISHED   1945
SECOND IMPRESSION 1946

PRINTED IN GREAT BRITAIN BY
CLARKE & SHERWELL LTD NORTHAMPTON
ON MELLOTEX BOOK PAPER MADE BY
TULLIS RUSSELL & CO LTD MARKINCH SCOTLAND

LIST OF ILLUSTRATIONS

PLATES IN COLOUR

BLACK AND WHITE ILLUSTRATIONS

'PAMELA WRITING A LETTER'
Detail from a painting by Joseph Highmore, 1740

LETTERS are valuable and entertaining in proportion to the wit and ability, and above all to the imprudence, of those who write them. For the merit of a really good letter is always colloquial; it is full of news or gossip, it is personal, unstudied and indiscreet. It shows the writer without his guards or defences, uncovers all his thoughts and feelings ; and that is why honest letters are more informative, more amusing, more pathetic, more vital than any considered autobiography. Of all documents these are the most essentially human. They bring us into a curiously intimate relation with men and women of the past, a relation sometimes exhilarating, sometimes nearly painful. Even when literary skill is absent, a passionate or vigorous expression, a trick of humour, is enough to produce an immediate sense of living personality. Some of the most intensely poignant letters (those of soldiers and explorers, for instance) are not infrequently those in which literary skill plays no part at all. And if letters too often reveal the dark and woeful caverns of the soul, they also reveal the bright, unlaced or playful aspects of outwardly pompous persons.

7

But it seems to me that we have to set up a distinction, however fluid or pliable it may seem to be in practice, between the English Letter Writers and the writers of English letters. This division is not by any means a literary artifice, nor is the subtle problem of category to be decided upon a basis of literary accomplishment. The English Letter Writers, properly speaking, are those men and women whose fame as writers of prose is chiefly or wholly dependent upon their published epistles. Of these, Lady Mary Wortley Montagu, Chesterfield and Horace Walpole are conspicuous and obvious types, and there can be no doubt of Cowper's position in the same category. The group is not a large one; it could have been assembled easily in a drawing-room of moderate size.

The case is very different in the second of our two categories. Everybody writes, everybody has written, letters; and so the task of making a small yet representative collection is one of immense difficulty, even if we restrict ourselves to the published writings of the eminent. And this is not enough. Like all other forms of writing, letters may be studied as modes profoundly typical of the periods in which they were composed, and in this respect the ordinary letters of ordinary people may have as much value as any others. Then again, we have our delightful English amusement of "writing to the papers." Here, of course, the letter is not really a letter at all, but simply a device whereby the writer may deodorise complaints and assert his important opinions. Are these to be excluded from the study of English letter-writing? Must we omit also the "open letter"—political diatribe in the style of Junius? And should there be no reference to the turgid epistolary novels of the eighteenth century?—for these reflect, with pompous or facetious accentuation, all the tricks, turns and habits of contemporary letter-writers. Finally there is the obscure though fascinating subject of those who scribble anonymously. The reader will be indulgent, I hope, if I allow myself a seemly degree of latitude—at any rate in my concluding observations.

Now, if we are to appreciate the style and informed elegance, the fervour and intimacy of the earlier letters (those written before the period of decline), we have to remember their place in the system of personal communication. Letters were the means of maintaining personal relations between people who were separated by what we should now regard as only short distances. The speed with which they could be conveyed, before the age of railways, depended upon the weather. It must also be remembered that personal visits, in the case of those who lived more than twenty miles apart, were very infrequent. After the decay of the Roman road-system in Britain there were scarcely any roads worthy of the name before 1800. The heavy coaches of the early eighteenth century lumbered, rolled and wallowed over deep-rutted and uneven tracks, frequently breaking their axles or falling over upon their sides. Riders or postboys were less dependent on the state of the tracks and the weather, but the number of horses

Sarah wife to John Duke
of Marlborough.

SARAH JENNINGS, DUCHESS OF MARLBOROUGH, 1660-1744
Oil painting by Sir Godfrey Kneller
By courtesy of Lord Spencer

SAMUEL JOHNSON, 1709-1784
Oil painting by Sir Joshua Reynolds
By courtesy of the Curators of the Bodleian Library

available for posting was not very considerable. (The first mail coach ran in 1784; by 1797 there were forty-two mail coach routes, and from this time onwards the speed of communication was greatly increased.) Letters thus played an important part in the lives of those who received and wrote them, an importance hardly conceivable to-day except in the case of people in distant lands and on active service.

And so, in leisurely polite ages, before these dismal days of improvement and invention, a letter was usually written with care and read with delight. It was not a conventional or slap-dash effusion; for grace, courtesy and accomplishment were always admired, even if they were not always present in a remarkable degree.

The importance of being elegant is not lightly to be disregarded. No doubt it is more important to be honest and amusing, but these virtues are greatly enhanced by elegance of style. That is why the eighteenth century is pre-eminently the age of the great English Letter Writers, as it is pre-eminently the age of great English conversation. Since then, after passing through a phase of perceptible decline, the arts of talking and writing in a familiar style have lamentably decayed, and the causes of decay are evident enough. Speedy communication, the hurry of life, complexity of employment, diversity of distraction, the press and the radio, increased irritability, a common resolve (it would seem) to destroy or contaminate all the sources of quiet, these are the factors which have now expelled our social graces and accomplishments. The greater part of what we do, perhaps the greater part of what we think, is hurried and ugly; fancy cannot spread her wings, and leisure and learning are pushed away by a brainless facility.

It is fashionable now-a-days to exhume the trivial and obscure, as though such a proceeding were evidence of superior taste. This may be done with little trouble. Of trifles and obscurity we have abundance. But I shall not apologise for devoting the major part of my space to the great letter-writers, the lovable, the eminent and the entertaining; and of these I can choose only a few. Nor shall I apologise if I choose largely from the writers of the eighteenth and early nineteenth centuries, for it was in these periods, as I believe, that the best of our English letters were written. It is sufficiently obvious that in so slender a volume my selection may seem arbitrary, but I venture to hope that it will be at least moderately representative. If the objection is made, that I have not even mentioned some of the most amusing letter-writers, I can only say that such an objection applies equally to more than one pretentious anthology.

Women have a way of preserving themselves in their letters which only a few men have ever been able to attain or even faintly to emulate. At all times, even in pompous ages, the candour, fluency and ease of our female correspondence make it singularly vivid and endearing. For this reason many of the writers who are presented in this essay are women; not because

PASTON HALL AND CHURCH
Engraving from Murray's edition of *The Paston Letters*, 1823

they are in every way the best letter-writers—I do not think this is the case—but because they are the most intensely personal, the most intuitive and observant.

The first familiar English letters which have been preserved are those of the Paston family, covering the period 1434-1509. The Pastons were Norfolk people of moderate importance, tenacious of property, and uncomfortably involved in the Wars of the Roses. They were not accomplished writers and the interest of their letters is to a large extent antiquarian. The family became extinct in 1732. But if the Pastons were unskilled in the art of writing, they were assiduous preservers of correspondence. The letters cannot be described as vivid or lively, but they are valuable and interesting because they show us how conventional, plain, educated people wrote to each other in the fifteenth century. Those touches which reveal personal character do not often occur, and many of the letters are concerned with wrangles over property and with mercenary bargaining for marriages. Urgency is often impressed upon the bearer (there was, of course, no regulated system of postal service) : "be this delivered in haste," "in right great haste," "in hasty wise." Many readers will be most interested in the domestic details. Margaret Paston, for example, writes to her husband in 1451: "I pray you heartily that ye will send me a pot of treacle in haste, for I have been right evil at ease and your daughter both, since that ye yeden hence, and one of the tallest young men of this parish lyeth sick and hath a great myrr." On another occasion she asks him for "some crossbows and wyndacs, to bind them with"; and again, "it were well done ye should do purvey a garnish or twain of pewter vessel." The power of the priesthood is well displayed in a letter sent in 1463 from the Abbot of Langley to Sir John Paston, who owed money to the church. "This thus kept from holy church," he warns him, "may not be without great peril of soul." Letters of tenderness and affection do not appear often in the series, but there is a touching love-letter from Margery Brews to young John Paston, "endited at Topcroft with full heavy heart" (1476).

Formality prevails in the Paston Letters in spite of occasional frolicsome notes. It prevails also in the letters of Roger Ascham (1515-1568), a gentle, pious man with a passion for bows and arrows. Nor can it be said that the published letters of Francis Bacon (1561-1626) are intimately personal documents. Most of them are concerned with State or judicial affairs. They contain some of the most magnificent epistolary prose in the language—for example, the letter written to Essex on the occasion of his taking over the Lord-Lieutenancy of Ireland in 1599—but they are essentially formal. And there is a disappointing austerity and aridity of style in the letters of that great master of harmonious prose, Sir Thomas Browne (1605-1682).

The earliest private letters which vividly display the writer's character are those of that entirely delightful woman, Dorothy Osborne. She was the daughter of Sir Peter Osborne, a Royalist, and she married in 1654 William (afterwards Sir William) Temple, whose father sat in the Long Parliament. It was in the Temples' house of Moor Park that Swift, employed as a secretary by Sir William, met the child Esther Johnson, or Stella.

When Dorothy was twenty-one she and her brother fell in with young Temple, who had left Cambridge without a degree and was on his way to France. This was in 1648, when Temple himself was only twenty. William's affection and admiration were excited by a curious episode. The party found themselves at an inn in the Isle of Wight, and young Osborne imprudently cut an inscription on the glass of one of the windows: "And Haman was hanged on the gallows they had prepared for Mordecai." Those were not happy days for the political joker; the Osbornes and Temple were promptly arrested and were brought before the Roundhead governor of the Island. Osborne's joke might have had most unpleasant consequences, had it not been for Dorothy, who at once declared that it was she who had cut the words on the pane. Whether he believed her or not, the governor was a gallant man and released the prisoners.

Dorothy, before her marriage, lived with her widowed father at Chicksands in Bedfordshire and looked after his house. The letters in which her charming nature is preserved so perfectly were written to Temple between 1652 and 1654. They are love letters of the gentler sort, in which there is neither passion nor extravagance, but the assurance of a quiet, steady affection, with occasional touches of wit. Their most immediate and observable qualities are those of candour and of natural grace. No obsession with literary artifice and with conventional requirement obscures their lucidity and freshness. Honesty comes first, and there is no tendency to conceal the dejection through which Dorothy passed in the autumn and winter of 1653. She herself has given a perfect definition of the ideal letter: "All letters, methinks, should be free and easy as one's discourse; not studied as an oration, nor made up of hard words like a charm"—and in her own practice this precept was admirably exemplified.

Her pastoral notes are charming: "I walk out into a common that lies hard by the house, where a great many young wenches keep sheep and cows, and sit in the shade singing of ballads . . ." When Temple is in London there are commissions for seals and orange-flower water, tweezers and essences; and a dog, a proper dog for a countrywoman: "A masty is handsomer to me than the most exact little dog that ever lady played withal." Temple does not seem to have been always considerate in the matter of writing. "Your last letter came like a pardon to one upon the block . . . and you would have both pitied and laughed at me if you could have seen how woodenly I entertained the widow, who came hither the day before." In one letter she describes the ideal husband—not "a travelled Monsieur, whose head is feathered inside and outside"—and in another there is a remarkable suggestion: "For my part, I think it were very convenient that all such as intend to marry should live together in the same house some years of probation." She was married on Christmas Day 1654, and she died early in 1695.

One might have expected remarkable letters from Donne, but those which have survived are disappointing: they are pompous and fulsome and reveal that obsequious, conventional aspect of Donne which occasionally mars the magnificence of his poetry. The letters of John Evelyn, too, are full of elegant affectations, as when he speaks about "phonocamptics" to Dr. Beale in 1668, and of "hyemation in Dover Street" to Pepys in 1692.

There is nothing of elegant affectation or of pomposity in the familiar letters of Swift (1667-1745). He was a man who could scarcely write anything—not even the briefest of notes—without a perfusion of his bitter, turbulent, whimsical genius. Yet Swift, as we see in the epistolary *Journal to Stella*, could be homely, tender and extremely playful. This vehemence and odd variety of personal expression make his letters both tragic and entertaining; for if there is nothing more delightful than the gaiety of some of his letters to Stella, there is nothing in literature to exceed the pathos of his later letters to Pope and to Mrs. Whiteway when he knew that he was passing down the long avenues of suffering and weakness into the shadows of mental night. Perhaps the *Journal to Stella* is the most extraordinary of all English epistolary collections. It consists of the letters (preserved by Swift

JONATHAN SWIFT, 1667-1745
Oil painting by Charles Jervas

himelf) written when Swift was busy with politics in London, from 1710 to
1713, to Esther Johnson and her friend Mrs. Rebecca Dingley in Dublin.
Literary gossips are ready enough still to cackle over Swift's relations with
Esther Johnson and over the problem of their mysterious marriage. This
gossip need not concern us here. It is enough to know that Swift was
attached romantically to this handsome and lively woman—alleged to have
been Temple's natural daughter.

Swift's London epistles to the Dublin ladies (for Mrs. Dingley was
decorously included) give the drollest account of his life, with political
gossip and odd fragments of information. They are characterised in a sin-
gular way by what has come to be known as "the little language." This has
been impatiently curtailed or deleted by earlier editors, and our full knowledge of it now depends upon twenty-five letters in the British Museum.
In the "little language," where abbreviations and capital letters are freely
used, the Dean appears as "Presto," the ladies are addressed as "logues,"
"dallars," "sollahs," "MD" (My Dears), and "Pdfr" (Poor dear fond
rogues); "your letter" becomes "oo rettle," and "conversation" is amazingly

13

ALEXANDER POPE, 1688-1744
Pencil drawing by Jonathan Richardson

transformed into "tonvelsasens." To some, this playfulness is infuriating; to others, it is pathological; to others it shows deliciously the gay and affectionate side of the Dean's nature. To most readers, I fancy, the notes on every-day life are the most engaging features of the *Journal*. For Swift recorded, with his own peculiar vivacity, the smallest of details: How he put on his new wig and went "o hoao, to visit Lady Worsley"; how he dined with Abingdon and was disgusted because the wine was poison, "his carps were raw and his candles tallow"; how there was "a mighty increase of dirty wenches in straw hats"; how he wants "a necessary woman" and is "as helpless as an elephant"—and so on.

His bantering letters to women are among the best ever written by Swift, though he was oddly restrained when he wrote to Vanessa (Stella's rival, Miss Vanhomrigh). In the later correspondence it is dreadful to observe how his rage against the world—in his view a world of triumphant rogues and honoured fools—is overcome by the dark and rising flood of melancholy. "Drown the world!" he cries bitterly in a letter to Pope in 1725. Seven years later he complains that "his poetical fountain is drained." In 1740 he wrote to Mrs. Whiteway: "I am so stupid and confounded that I cannot express the mortification I am under both in body and mind." He died in October 1745.

Pope, a man of artifice, never shows the huge exuberance which is typical of Swift's genius, and apart from a little stilted coyness in his letters to the Misses Blount there is not much in his correspondence which can be described as animated. Like Swift, he was appalled by the victories of dullness. But he expressed himself in concentrations of brilliant and elaborate satire, unsurpassed in proficiency, very different from the manly bludgeoning or bellowing of the Dean. To me, at any rate, the most attractive thing in his letters is his deep affection for his mother—for here, if nowhere else, he was unreservedly sincere.

At one time Pope was the pompous friend and afterwards the venomous enemy of Lady Mary Wortley Montagu (1689-1762). If we are looking only for entertainment, Lady Mary is the Queen of English letter-writers. Accomplished, witty and eccentric, she was a woman of brisk intelligence and unconventional style. Her father was Evelyn Pierrepont, who in 1690 became the fifth Earl of Kingston.

Lady Mary married a dull but honourable gentleman, the friend of Addison, Edward Wortley Montagu, who received the appointment of Ambassador to the Porte in 1716. She accompanied him in his long and rather hazardous journey to Constantinople, and her letters written during this journey and from the Embassy are among the best that she wrote. Her

POPE'S VILLA AT TWICKENHAM
Oil painting by Samuel Scott

15

LADY MARY WORTLEY MONTAGU
Engraving by T. Cadell, 1790

descriptions are unequalled in lively and accurate detail. In her accounts
of people she is often gaily unscrupulous, her airs and anecdotes are sometimes those of a rake, and it is impossible not to observe traces of mas-
culinity in her approach to women and in her views of life in general. A
large proportion of her earlier letters were written to her sister the Countess
of Mar, and about an equal proportion of the later ones to her daughter
the Countess of Bute.

Her letters to Wortley Montagu before their marriage are composed
with unusual deliberation, though by no means devoid of candour. They
are obviously those of a woman whose emotions were never powerful. Her
affection for Wortley seems to have been always temperate, and in 1739,
after twenty-seven years of irreproachable married life, she left him and
settled in Italy. Here she remained for twenty-two years, returning after
Wortley's death in 1761, and herself dying in 1762. Lady Mary has a place
in the history of medical advance, for she introduced the simple method of
inoculation against the small-pox which she had seen employed in Turkey
in 1717.

Brilliance in superficial description, vivacity and veracity, are the out-
standing qualities of her style, and a lack of conventional reticence. In the
Jesuits' church at Cologne (1716) she deplores the jewels wasted "in the
adornment of rotten teeth and dirty rags," and she laughs at Nuremberg

16

when she sees the figure over the altar "in a fair full-bottomed wig very well powdered." The sight of the Turkish ladies in the hot baths at Sofia ("the women's coffee-house") caused her to reflect that "if it were the fashion to go naked, the face would be hardly observed." The women of Turkey, she says, have far more liberty than those of England, and the great ladies "seldom let their gallants know who they are." Her account of her visit to the Kiyaya's lady is luscious in the extreme and is timidly bowdlerised by popular editors. After her return to England we find her complaining of the prevalence of stupidity, "which is certainly owing to the coldness of this vile climate," and in 1726 she announces with regret "I insensibly dwindle into a spectatress." Most of her later letters are written from Lovere in Venetian territory, where she made her summer residence, delighting in her gardens, woods and arbours and "a dining-room of verdure capable of holding a table of twenty covers." From Venice, at the age of seventy-one, she could say that she was "ready to sing her 'Nunc dimittis' with pleasure."

Among the correspondents of Lady Mary was the formidable Sarah Jennings, Duchess of Marlborough. But some recently published letters (*Letters of a Grandmother*, edited by Gladys Scott Thomson, 1943) show us the more affectionate side of this fretful and energetic woman, and are, indeed, full of tenderness. And yet Sarah was always impatient, and when she was not exasperated by people she was exasperated by architecture.

VIEW OF CONSTANTINOPLE IN 1721
Engraving from *Nouvelle Description de la Ville de Constantinople*, Paris, 1721

The Assembly Room at York, she declares, "exceeds all the nonsense and madness that I ever saw"; and she comes to the conclusion that there is "some tincture more or less of madness in almost everybody that one knows." These letters, written between 1732 and 1735, are eminently commendable; they are edited with real scholarship and are presented in a charming form.

The eighteenth century was an age of involved elegance. To call it artificial would be far too crude an analysis, for it certainly aimed at a real transformation or standard of character. Manners were not everything, for monkeys might have manners, but the gentleman was dedicated from his birth to the service of the Graces. Without their divine assistance he could never hope to wear a wig or carry a sword or snap a snuff-box like a man of the highest fashion. "The Graces, the Graces! remember the Graces!" cries Chesterfield to his unhopeful son; and this indeed was the cry of tutors, fathers, mothers, masters and all who had the care of elegant youth.

It is a little odd, perhaps pathetic, that Chesterfield, himself the perfect exponent of social grace, was a short and ugly man, with a big head, thick eyebrows, and a most unpleasantly cynical expression. His famous letters to his natural son, Philip Stanhope, give us, in the form of instruction and advice, a portrait of the ideal gentleman of the eighteenth century. Philip, awkward and shy, was never able to profit from letters and example; perhaps they overwhelmed him and he would have done better without them. But Chesterfield's letters, for us, have a peculiar value and are richly entertaining. The obtuse ferocity of Johnson was never more foolishly directed than it was when he denounced them in a well-known sentence which is both brutal and entirely inappropriate. For it was Chesterfield's wish that his Philip should be a gentleman and a man of honour: not a mean character, or one which has ever been common. It is amusing, if, again, it is not pathetic, to find him beginning with pompous discourses on oratory to a little boy of seven. But the bulk of the letters are those which were sent to Philip when he was abroad, from 1747 to 1754, studying or travelling. He must always court the Graces. He must overcome his "curious infelicity of diction." He must learn to "distinguish carefully between the pleasures of a man of fashion and the vices of a scoundrel." There is much difference, both in method and in consequences. "In love, a man may lose his heart with dignity; but if he loses his nose, he loses his character into the bargain." He would have no excuse for being sordidly profligate, especially in Paris "where gallantry is both the profession and the practice of every woman of fashion"—or, as we read later, "where so many women of fashion generously serve as volunteers." Well may the old cynic observe "I have seldom or never written to you upon the subject of Religion and Morality." These may be left more properly to the tutor, Mr. Harte, or to the voice of reason. Yet the purity of the moral character (and here Chesterfield has something perfectly definite in his mind, even if it is only a code required by his

eternal Graces) is a part of the gentleman's outfit and is to be jealously guarded.

Chesterfield's letters could only have been written in the eighteenth century, and only in the first half of it. They represent the type and image of something which could only then have been evolved and which was definitely and exclusively the product of a period. This applies equally to the charming but little-known letters of William Shenstone (1714-1763).

William Shenstone was a minor poet and essayist who inherited a small estate known as the Leasowes in Shropshire. Here he devoted himself to all the joys of landscape gardening, until the Leasowes became a place of great local renown. He was a simple creature, happy in retirement, who preferred honesty "to lace, brocade and the smiles of the ladies." Ordinary talk gave him "no more pleasure than the canking of a goose or the quacking of a duck." He knew that his advantages were not "eminently shining," but they suited "his particular humour." His placid enjoyment was found in pillars and shrubberies and crooked walks, in groves and in flowers. Let the world rage as it might: "I feed my wild-ducks and I water my carnations." He wrote frequently to Lady Luxborough, the sister of Bolingbroke, who was also a most enthusiastic gardener. There is much talk of altars, lyres and wreaths, knots and Roman reeds, festoons and walls and pedestals and other "rural embellishments." He destroys his "little Pavilion in the water," because he prefers it as a ruin, and advises her

HORACE WALPOLE, 4th EARL OF ORFORD, 1717-1797
Lithograph after a drawing by Sir Thomas Lawrence

ladyship to set up a "gothick skreen" of wood. "I hope your Ladyship is now planting furiously . . . Why don't your Ladyship throw all your Haystacks into the Form of Pyramids?"

What Shenstone did at the Leasowes, Horace Walpole did more grandly at Strawberry Hill. He would have hated comparison with a man he described so contemptuously as "that water-gruel bard."

Horace Walpole (1717-1797) was the third son of Sir Robert. "A trifling chap after all" was the opinion of Thomas Creevey; but, in the more recent and more valuable opinion of Professor Saintsbury, "It is questionable whether . . . we have in English any superior to him as a letter-writer." No doubt he was a trivial creature, whose tame Gothic and elegant imitations (paper tiles among them) exasperate the man of sturdy sense. But no writer has ever depicted his times with greater brilliance or malice or in such vital colours. If Walpole's letters had been the sole surviving

20

THE CHAPEL IN THE GARDEN AT STRAWBERRY HILL
Engraving by Godfrey after Pars

documents of the eighteenth century, we should still have a more vivid idea of that period than of any other phase in the social history of England. Civically idle, he was busy enough in arranging, preserving and enlarging the pattern of his own life; a moderate scholar; a miscellaneous writer of great ability; a wit and a gossip; and above all things a man whose gift of description in familiar letters is absolutely unsurpassed. No one who has read them can ever forget his accounts of the trial and execution of the rebel Scots Lords (1746), of the Peace Festival at Ranelagh (1749), of an evening with gay company at Vauxhall (1750), of the funeral of George II (1760), of Wesley in his Bath chapel (1766), and of the air-balloon (1784). These are but a few examples. Walpole wrote thousands of letters, and he certainly wrote the best of them with a definite, a conscious literary intention.

If Chesterfield and Walpole represented, in their different ways, the perfection of elegance, Johnson is to be regarded as the great man who stood

21

up for the Rights of Rudeness. He was the antidote to the foppery of the age. Johnson paralysed most of the people he met, and he still seems to paralyse those who write about him. Noise, bulk and authority, his massive body and his growling voice, his brutal retorts and immovable prejudice, inspired some with admiration, others with terror, and others with pardonable dislike. Our knowledge of the lighter, kinder aspects of Johnson depends very largely upon his letters, particularly those written to Mrs. Thrale (before the Piozzi quarrel) and her daughter Queeney. Yet even here we have the rumblings of solemn platitude and of ponderous admonition. Queeney is to "make all her figures with critical exactness," and she is never "to acquiesce in total vacuity." In writing to his "honoured Mistress" he could relax more freely—far more freely than he ever did when writing to Boswell. He could reveal the dark and invading terrors which oppressed him, his "gloomy discontent and importunate distress," but he could also expand in moods of real jocosity. Thus, in 1777, he devotes nearly half a letter to his joy at learning that she is to give up her wig. "We will burn it and get drunk," he announces. But (so inveterate the practice of giving advice)—"do not take too much time in combing, and twisting, and papering, and unpapering, and curling, and frizzing, and powdering, and getting out the powder, with all the other operations required in the cultivation of a head of hair." There is nothing to equal the pathos of the letters which he wrote "in no cheerful solitude" when he knew that Mrs. Thrale was tired of him; nothing to equal the tragic, terrified impertinence which he displayed on the occasion of her marriage to Piozzi. Of Johnson's place among the great letter-writers there may well be some doubt. His letters are deeply impressed by the revolutions of his tortured and irritable nature; their value is almost exclusively personal; they do not abound in lively anecdotes and entertaining description like those of Walpole and of Lady Mary.

One is tempted to wonder what Johnson would have thought of Boswell if he could have seen his letters to Temple, and above all if he could have seen the papers privately and luxuriously presented, some years ago, by Colonel Isham. Nobody can ever have received stranger letters than those which the Rev. William Temple received from his friend, the "ancient Scots gentleman" (published in 1924 by Professor Tinker). They display, without any shame and without very much art, all the squalor, follies, vanities, mawkish regrets and futile resolutions of Boswell's unedifying life. To the ribald they are doubtless amusing; to the charitable they are infinitely sad; to the alienist they reveal a state of mind which is chiefly due to venereal disorder intensified by habitual drunkenness. His indulgence plunged him into melancholy, his melancholy threw him back into renewed indulgence. And so the fearful alternations continue. He keeps "a dear infidel" for his "hours of Paphian bliss." A little later, and he vows that "upon my honour, I shall be moral for the future." He is "exalted in piety."

'THE NINE LIVING MUSES OF GREAT BRITAIN'

Mrs. Sheridan in the centre; (r.) Angelica Kauffmann with Elizabeth Carter and Anna Barbauld;
(l.) Charlotte Lennox, Catherine Macaulay, Elizabeth Griffith, Miss More and Mrs. Montagu

He is "too dissipated and drinks too much wine." At last, "I fly to every mode of agitation." The "sure prospect of death" is "frightful." But three years after the death of his wife he had "several matrimonial schemes." The more one knows of Boswell the more convinced one is of the immense debt that we owe to Malone as one of the chief producers of the *Life of Johnson.*

Sterne (1713-1768) wrote letters of sentiment, usually fulsome, to various women. He told Mrs. Vesey that she was "a System of Harmonic Vibrations"; to Lady Warkworth he protested that her eyes and lips had "turned a man into a fool"; to his dear Eliza (Mrs. Draper) he described his eating of a "Chicking"—"with Tears, a bitter Sause." All very sad; and yet he could cynically alter, for Eliza's benefit, the draft of a letter which he had composed some years previously for another woman.

Sentiment, or the extraction of a romantic essence from things apparently trivial, was a literary invention of the eighteenth century, owing much (in this country) to the example and the writings of Sterne himself. One might have anticipated a powerful infusion of this new sensibility in the letters of ladies; but this is not the case. Women in their letters, as I have pointed out, are more concerned with immediate personal expression

23

than with literary form and artifice. And we have, in the latter half of the eighteenth century, a vast and embarrassing mass of female correspondence.

A great deal of this correspondence was produced by the little society which came to be known, soon after 1750, as the Blue Stockings. The centre of this group was Mrs. Elizabeth Montagu, at whose elegant Athenian house in Portman Square literary ladies assembled for talk and intellectual pleasures. They did not wear blue stockings: the stockings which gave their name to this polite and learned society were those of Mr. Stillingfleet, an early frequenter. Hester Chapone, Mrs. Carter, Mrs. Ord, Mrs. Vesey, Mrs. Boscawen were conspicuous among the original Blues, and there were always hangers-on, such as Mrs. Delany, the Duchess of Portland, the Duchess of Beaufort, Lady Radnor and Lady Onslow. It is wrong to describe Mrs. Thrale, the exasperating friend of Dr. Johnson, as a genuine Blue Stocking, although she was at one time patronised by Mrs. Montagu. But the term "Blue Stocking," or merely "Blue," was gradually applied without discrimination to any female who professed learning or literature.

An excellent selection of Blue Stocking letters, artlessly edited by Lady Llanover, will be found in the *Life and Correspondence* of Mrs. Delany. Two charming volumes of Mrs. Boscawen's letters have been published in recent years by Aspinall-Oglander, and two volumes of Mrs. Montagu's letters are available—one edited in 1906 by Climenson, and the other in 1923 by Blunt. Of Mrs. Thrale's letters, the most revealing (and revolting) are those published in 1934 by the late Marquis of Lansdowne; the letters written by this appalling woman to her daughter Queeney. "My loveliest Tit" of 1780 has become "Dear Miss Thrale" by 1787. There is a gentle charm, always faintly smug, in the letters of Mrs. Delany, which are chiefly valuable as records of ladylike occupations extended over a long period.

Very frequently it is the lighter social letters of any given period which are the most informative, for they throw an unpremeditated accent upon details which a more solemn or pretentious writer is not likely to observe at all. This is true of the letters, for example, of Lady Sarah Lennox (1745-1826), the lovely girl who might have been Queen of England. Everyone knows how the Prince of Wales (afterwards George III) fell in love with her when she was fifteen and he was overcome, or nearly so, by "a daily increasing admiration of the fair sex." Her own feelings or designs (if she had any) are not clear, but she certainly despised the fatuous and unhappy young George. "The hipocrite had the face to come up & speak to me with all the good humour in the world . . . his behaviour is that of a man who has neither *sense*, *good nature*, nor *honesty*." She repelled him with cold indignation and in their subsequent meetings was almost impertinently brief: but she was one of the bridesmaids at his wedding in 1761 and was, according to Walpole, "by far the chief angel." At the age of seventeen she married Thomas Charles Bunbury, the race-horse owner, left him in 1769 and lived

24

LADY HENRIETTA FRANCES SPENCER, COUNTESS OF BESSBOROUGH, 1761-1821
Coloured engraving by Francesco Bartolozzi after the drawing by Lavinia, Countess Spencer
By courtesy of the Trustees of the British Museum

LAURENCE STERNE, 1713-1768
Coloured drawing by L. Carmontelle. Musée Condé, Chantilly

for a while with her cousin, Lord William Gordon, and in 1781 married George Napier and became the mother of three famous soldiers. Her letters are full of light social gossip and ingenious observations, with a sprinkling of current slang. "I have given you a pretty good boar upon dress," she says, after a long account of clothes and hair-dressing. At the time of the American War she wrote "I don't love Presbetiryans & I love the English soldiers"; but in 1777 she declared that she was glad she was not the Queen after all, for she would have gone mad to think that a person she loved was "the cause of such a shameful war."

Certainly we find in this one century alone an enchanting, bewildering abundance of letters; and among them, as I think, are the best letters that were ever written in our language. Some, like those of Walpole, are notable for shining veracity of description; others, like those of Swift, for an instant and overwhelming effusion of personality; and others, like those of Shenstone, for a blending of sensibility and artifice. But I have as yet said nothing of the man whose letters perhaps exceed all the others in beauty of style, in exquisite pathos and in luminous portrayal—William Cowper.

Cowper was a man whose gentle mind was cruelly tormented by apprehensions of a religious nature; or perhaps it would be more accurate to say that he was a man whose recurring melancholy made him the prey of the gloomier theological ideas which in his time were almost the only indications of religious vitality. He was from childhood a sensitive and withdrawing creature, and yet, when happy, he could be the gayest of companions. He found his refuge and his comfort in the placid affection of Mrs. Unwin and in the retired enjoyment of rural delights. Yet there were times when the darker powers of his mental conflict wore him down and he knew the invading and overmastering terrors of insanity.

No English letters are more exquisitely written, none are less artificial or more lucidly sincere than those of Cowper. They give him a high place, not merely among letter-writers but among the great masters of English prose; and as autobiography there is nothing to surpass them. Cowper wrote without pains and with all the uncourted felicity of genius. He had no thought of the circulation or publication of his letters; indeed, he would have dreaded and resented nothing more bitterly. But it may be doubted whether, on account of these very letters, his position as a prose writer is not as high as, if not higher than, his position as a poet. "What Nature expressly designed me for I have never been able to conjecture," he wrote to William Unwin in 1781, and it is observable that he did not seriously set about his work as a poet (mainly for the sake of distraction) until he was nearly fifty. The letters which he wrote when he was living with Mrs. Unwin at Olney—with Lady Austen, capricious angel, passing through the scene—reveal Cowper in all his moods. He could play at battledore and shuttlecock with Lady Austen, or he could find seclusion in the greenhouse "where only my myrtles presume to peep in at the window." And how delightful the picnic in "the Spinnie," a charming wilderness belonging to Mrs. Throckmorton of Weston. In fearful contrast are the letters written to Bull or Newton in which he describes the onset of melancholy. "Loaded as my life is with despair, I have no such comfort as would result from a supposed probability of better things to come, were it once ended." Nor has he fallen yet (in 1784) into the lowest abyss of the mental tragedy. That is revealed in the heartrending letters which he wrote, between 1795 and 1799, to his cousin Lady Hesketh. He died in 1800.

No one will disagree with Saintsbury when he says that "the eighteenth century is the century of the letter with us." In this period of a hundred years more good letters were written than at any other time in our history. But, in spite of the somewhat overestimated shock of the French Revolution and all the tawdry innovations of an industrial age, the habits of the eighteenth century flowed on into the nineteenth without any swift reduction or decay.

This observation is well illustrated by the gay gossip of Thomas Creevey (1768-1838), one of the most industrious and exuberant of letter-writers. Himself a person of no great importance, he knew most of the important people of his times, and he wrote thousands of letters with cheerful malice and happy indiscretion. Lady Holland, in 1812, did not hesitate to describe him as a "mischievous toad." It is for this reason that his editors, prudent or prudish, have given us only a relatively small fraction of his vast correspondence.

Creevey was known as the son of a Liverpool merchant, although scandal said that he was actually the son of the first Earl of Sefton. In 1802 he was nominated by the Duke of Norfolk to the pocket borough of Thetford, and in 1806 he was Secretary to the Board of Control. In 1820 he became the Member for Appleby through the patronage of the Earl of Thanet; later, Grey appointed him to one of the Ordnance offices, and Melbourne gave him the Treasurership of Greenwich Hospital, where he was equally pleased with "Corinthian Pillars" and "two perfect water-closets." Although essentially trifling, Creevey was not without abilities of moderate value; he had graduated M.A. in 1792 and was called to the Bar in 1794. He married a widow, Mrs. Ord, and his step-daughter Elizabeth became his favourite correspondent.

As light and lively social documents, perpetually twinkling with nimble wit and well spiced with irony, there is nothing so good as Creevey's letters. For Creevey had the pen of the ideal gossip. He respected people only on account of their worth or charm, never on account of their rank. To him the Earl of Carlisle was Gooserump, George III was Old Nobs, Palmerston was Cupid, Lord John Russell was Pie and Thimble, the Countess of Darlington was The Pop, and Princess Lieven, The Snipe; while Brougham had a string of opprobious names—Beelzebub, Wickedshifts, Bruffam, Guy Vaux. In his own circle he was affectionately known

WILLIAM COWPER, 1731-1800
Engraving by Blake after Lawrence

as Diddy or Nummy. For some time (up to 1811) he was the friend of
Prinney—the Prince of Wales—and saw the glories of the Brighton Pavilion.
More than once he was "a little bosky." His letters give rare views of the
machinery and the machinations of politics; but he was an honest man, and
he admits that the discovery of such things "dreadfully diminishes one's
parliamentary amusement." He was in Brussels when Waterloo was fought,
and after the battle he personally congratulated the Duke, who observed
"It has been a damned serious business." In 1820 he was present in the
House of Lords during the trial of Queen Caroline, where he wrote a
running commentary for the benefit of Miss Ord. Outside the House were
crowds giving cheers for the Queen and hoots for the Duke of Wellington,
and a mob of marching sailors. It was devilish hot when Brougham was
making his great oration in Caroline's defence, and so Creevey and his
friends went out for a walk on Westminster Bridge. In February 1821 he
dined with the unfortunate but altogether horrible Queen and observed
that she was "more stately and much more agreeable." She died in August

27

with considerable dignity, overcome by immense doses of calomel and of castor oil.

Upon the resignation of Grey in 1832, Creevey (then sixty-four) remarked of himself and his party: "Dead as mutton, every man John of us, so help me Jingo!" But he was undismayed, in reality, by political events. He found his pleasure in the small episodes of life and its lighter tattle. Thus (in 1833), "I have for the first time boarded an omnibus, and it is really charming." He notes how the servants all knelt round the billiard table when Lord Derby read prayers, and how, at Lambton, a party was disturbed when the gas went out. "Was there ever?" he chirrups after some particularly good anecdote. "It was really *too*!" He lived to see the accession of Queen Victoria, whom he admired greatly and whom he described as "a handy little Vic."

Another delightful correspondent (though a very different one) who crosses the bridge between the eighteenth and nineteenth centuries is Lady Bessborough, the sister of the Duchess of Devonshire and the mother of Lady Caroline Lamb. We know her chiefly through her correspondence with Lord Granville Leveson Gower (1773-1846). She was thirty-two when she first saw Granville, a beautiful youth of twenty, at Naples in 1794. There is no doubt that he fell in love with her; no doubt that she gave him in return a deeply romantic affection which endured until the day of her death, although she at once assured him that she was "old enough and wise enough to be certain of never again involving herself in the misery of feeling more than the common Interest of friendship for any one." Left largely to her own devices by a dull husband, with whom she temperately quarrelled, those devices were innocent and often gently intellectual: she read Milton, she studied Lavater, drew, played the piano. She had the gift of attracting the friendship and the confidence of men, as well as of arousing their more troublesome emotions. There was a most embarrassing scene at a ball in 1805 when Sheridan, very drunk, openly protested that "she was the only person he had ever really loved"; and another scene in 1809 when she was tempestuously courted (in private) by the Prince of Wales, and saw, partly with horror partly with amusement, "that immense, grotesque figure flouncing about half on the couch half on the ground." At this time she was forty-eight and the Prince forty-seven.

Her letters to Granville show all the nobility of an affection that was always intense, although never passionate. She admitted that she would "feel pain," but no regret, when he "attached himself to any one." She upbraids him quietly for short letters and silence. Her solicitude was unvarying. When he moved the Address in the House of Commons she advised him to prepare himself by taking sal volatile and camphor julep. When he stood upright while driving his curricle she told him how she hated it. But the interest of her letters is by no means exclusively romantic. They illuminate the fringes of history. She was in Paris in 1802 and was

KING GEORGE III, 1738-1820
Coloured chalk drawing by D. Hamilton, 1769

present at a ball given by Madame Récamier when the hostess, who fancied herself in recumbent positions, allowed the visitors to see her in bed. She dined with Talleyrand, she talked with Berthier, who spoke of the "nullité invincible du Roi." Police were taking down the Caps of Liberty from the churches and were replacing the crucifixes. There were spies everywhere. She saw Napoleon at a review "on a fine old white Horse of the late King's," and observed that "his glory faded the moment he passed his own troops . . . never was there any character that united such contrasts of greatness and littleness." In 1805 she acted as hostess at the Brighton Pavilion in the absence of Mrs. Fitzherbert, who was ill. In 1808 she wrote a gloriously funny account of Dublin society. In 1815, at Marseilles, she made friends with Masséna; and in the same year, at Genoa, she described the Princess of Wales: "a short, very fat, elderly woman, with an extremely red face . . . in a Girl's white frock . . . quite low (disgustingly so), down to the middle of her stomach; very black hair and eyebrows." And throughout her letters we have a natural and intimate account of life among the aristocratic families and in the great houses of Britain.

Both Creevey and Lady Bessborough knew and admired that "noble animal," Charles James Fox (1749-1806), the kindly and exuberant reprobate whose genius and honesty give him a place of pre-eminent singularity among our statesmen. His letters are remarkable; particularly, I think, the letters which he wrote when his vast energies were declining and he had retired with Mrs. Armistead (whom he married in 1795) to the seclusion of St. Ann's Hill. Here he delighted in thorns and elms and nightingales, in the westerly wind and the sunshine, and in all the simple joys of a rural estate. "We are now here for good," he wrote in 1803, "and beautiful and delightful it is beyond measure." No man had ever spent himself more furiously in the strenuous enjoyment of life, or fought more nobly in the turmoil of politics, than Fox; and there are no letters from retirement which have a gentler charm, a more serene philosophy, than his.

Towards the end of the eighteenth century and in the early decades of the nineteenth a new and vital movement in literature was establishing modes of its own. This is the age of what is described, with only partial accuracy and with pedantic insistence, as the Romantic Revival. Foremost among the poets were Shelley, Keats, Byron, Coleridge and Wordsworth; while Scott may perhaps be regarded as more definitely transitional; and elegant or imaginative prose was brilliantly represented by Lamb, De Quincey, Hazlitt, Walter Savage Landor, Thomas Love Peacock. The letters of Byron, Scott and Lamb are certainly admirable—those of the first two on account of their freedom and energy, and those of Lamb on account of their grace and invention.

But the letters of Keats are particularly remarkable, for he was a poet who could write about poetry in a style unequalled by any other man, and there are many—many among poets at any rate—who would not hesitate to say that his letters are among the best in our language. With Keats, vision was never lost in obscurity or scattered in symbolic utterance (as with Blake); he could write lucidly and with all the precision of true genius upon the very nature of the poet himself. Thus, in the famous letter written to Woodhouse in 1818, he shows that the "poetical Character" is a thing without limits or constant attributes: "It has no self—it is everything and nothing . . . What shocks the virtuous philosopher, delights the cameleon Poet. . . A Poet is the most unpoetical of any thing in existence, because he has no Identity." He himself is aware of the "very fact" that he has "no nature"; he is perpetually in other bodies and other modes of being. When he is in contact with other people he feels that he is "annihilated." Reality, for him, was never objective: the one reality, the light of his mind, was poetic vision. "The faint conception I have of Poems to come brings the blood frequently into my forehead." He hopes that he "may not lose all interest in human affairs," that his acuteness of vision will never be injured by his indifference to mere praise. "But even now I am perhaps not speaking for myself: but for some character in whose soul I now live."

Such letters as those of Keats—if there are any comparable—stand in a class of their own and have no more in common with ordinary loquacious

JOHN KEATS, 1795-1821
Drawing by B. R. Haydon

epistles (however excellent) than ordinary talk has with poetry. Under the heading of ordinary loquacious epistles we must include those of Scott, but he was in many ways a splendid letter-writer with a free-and-easy manly style, and it is possible that many readers to-day would prefer his letters to his novels and his poems. When he writes merrily to Miss Edgeworth about the plovers' eggs and the champagne in London, or sadly to Cadell, his publisher, about the giving up of his daily cigar and his mountain dew, or when he is facetious about the sketching lady who "drew like cart-horses," he conveys an immediate sense of his charming and unaffected personality. Lamb is more consciously a writer. One cannot say that he,

31

like Sir Walter, was unaffected. His loving descriptions of London prove the contrary; and in writing to Coleridge on the subject of a sucking-pig he asks him whether the eyes "came away kindly with no Oedipean avulsion."

The letters of Wordsworth are kindly, modest, long and eminently sensible: the best of them, I think, are those written during his travels in 1837. But William as a letter-writer falls far behind his remarkable sister, Dorothy. This exquisitely sensitive woman was the lifelong companion of the poet, who said that she "gave him eyes." Dorothy had the nature and the eyes of a poet, but she was domestic too, and we find her continually looking after William and always attending to homely things—as, for example, the "smoke disperser" in De Quincey's cottage.

To turn from this gentleness to the fiery turbulence and theatrical energy of Byron is like passing from a quiet room into the full blast of a tempest. The flame and force, the mental conflict and agonising pride, the humour and extravagance of this diabolical genius are nowhere so vividly displayed as in his letters. There are none with a more vehement personal quality, none which are more likely either to shock the reader or to hold his amazed attention. For Byron was a man without any unvarying bias or polarity, and it is doubtful whether he could ever be, or ever wished to be, sincere. He sits up until four in the morning playing at hazard, but writes to his mother "my nature leads me to solitude." He was probably nearer the truth when he wrote to Murray, "I could never live but for one human being at any time" (1819). Everyone knows of his affection for his little daughter, but he could say to Augusta Leigh: "I don't know what Scrope Davies meant by telling you I liked Children, I abominate the sight of them so much that I have always had the greatest respect for the character of Herod." He told Henry Drury that the Greeks were "plausible rascals," who had "all the Turkish vices without their courage." But he gave his last energies and his life in the struggle for Greek liberation. Byron is a man outside or beyond all categories, all conventional assessment. He is always moving, always changing, will not sit for his portrait and has defeated every biographer. It is only in the poem of *Don Juan*, and above all in these letters, that his ardent and elusive nature becomes occasionally tangible.

If Byron could never be sincere it was because he always considered, in essentially dramatic terms, the effect of his words or gestures, not only upon others but also upon himself. In this respect he was by no means unique, nor can it be said that the postures of inverted egoism are peculiar to men. But it is only in the letters (and the journals) of women that we find all the tragic fullness, the passionate unburdening, of real candour. No one can read the letters of Charlotte Brontë (1816-1855), unfolding phase by phase the melancholy story of her life, without being aware that such reading is a painful experience.

CHARLES JAMES FOX, 1749-1806
Enamel on copper by Henry Bone after the painting by John Opie
By gracious permission of H.M. The King

BRIGHTON PAVILION
Coloured engraving by John Nash, 1827

Motherless from girlhood, Charlotte was brought up in Haworth parsonage by a dyspeptic and unsociable father, who relieved his irritation by the firing of pistols. The only happiness that she knew was in the companionship of her sisters, Ann and Emily. Her wretched brother, Patrick Branwell, can have been little comfort to any of them. Emily and Branwell died in 1848; Ann died in the following year. At the age of thirty-eight (1854) Charlotte married her father's curate, Nicholls. Her marriage was placidly happy, but her health was already broken and she died in 1855. Of her letters (all are admirably presented in the *Shakespeare Head Brontë*) the most moving are those written to her friend Ellen Nussey. They are unequalled in poignant revelation. Darkness was planted in her mind, as with Cowper, by religious fears in youth. "Do not think that I am good," she wrote; "I only wish to be so." She was in a state of "horrid, gloomy uncertainty." When only twenty-one she was afflicted by "evil, wandering thoughts" and wondered if the "ghastly Calvinistic doctrines" were true. "If Christian perfection be necessary to salvation, I shall never be saved;

THE MAIN STREET, HAWORTH
Engraving by Arthur North, 1884

33

my heart is a very hotbed for sinful thoughts." Then came the trials of a governess, intolerable to her sensitive nature. After this, a period of some easement and relief in Brussels; and then "something in me, which used to be enthusiasm, is tamed down and broken . . . I no longer regard myself as young—indeed, I shall soon be twenty-eight." One can understand why she thought Miss Austen a pretty trifler. "Miss Austen," she said, "is only shrewd and observant." But Charlotte herself was never lacking in shrewdness. "Lord Derby's 'Christian love and spirit'," she wrote in 1852, "is worth three half-pence farthing." The pathos of her last letters—those written in February 1855 when her life was fading—is indescribable. They cannot be made the object of cursory quotation.

The same unequivocal sincerity is to be found in the letters of Jane Welsh Carlyle (1801-1866), the wife of Thomas Carlyle. From her infancy she was brisk, intelligent and imperious, but the presence of a morbid or neurotic element in her nature is unquestionable. At the age of ten she burnt her doll on a funeral pyre, and when she was fourteen she wrote a tragedy. Frequent headaches in later life were relieved by the drinking of tea and the smoking of cigarettes. The grace and wit of her earlier style give place to a querulous vivacity, but her letters are among the most eminently readable of their period. They show in a pleasant and entirely convincing way her affection for her husband and her attention to domestic detail. Until 1844 she ordered his clothes at the tailor's, and all went well until she produced a sky-blue coat with yellow buttons. In 1836 she went on her first railway journey (to Liverpool) and wrote from the hotel, "O Darling, thank heaven that we are without bugs." Her meeting with D'Orsay in his "invisible inexpressibles" evokes a comparison with Carlyle in his grey plaid suit. Often she gives maliciously brilliant accounts of the people she met, and her description of Mrs. Gaskell is noteworthy—"a very kind cheery woman in her own house; but there is an atmosphere of moral dullness about her, as about all Socinian women." One does not gather that she was ever miserable, in spite of that cry of irony: "Oh men! men! how stupid you are in your dealings with us poor egg-shell wretches!"

Elizabeth Barrett Browning (1806-1861) takes a high place among the women letter-writers of the nineteenth century. Her style is quiet, simple and assured, for she was a happy woman. When she wrote to her sister from Italy, describing her life with Robert, she always conveyed a delightful impression of serenity and of well-being. Even after her illness in March 1848 it was not long before she was "pouring out the coffee, and as impertinent as usual." The Brownings were seldom shaken by historical events, but they were in Paris during Louis Napoleon's coup d'état in 1851. This horrible episode, with its bloodshed and ruin, did not affect them very deeply. "The people never rose," declares Elizabeth,—"it was nothing but a little popular scum, cleared off at once by the troops." And she adds casually, "Painful of course." It is not often that she speaks of dress and

THOMAS CARLYLE, 1795-1881
Drawing by Walter Greaves

the usual feminine affairs, though she notes at Paris in 1858 that "Petti-coats are still comprehensive and hoops regnant." Robert himself, except in his love letters, had a less felicitous epistolary style.

But, in the forcible and even strident expression of character, none of the Victorians could ever surpass the Queen herself. She wrote incessantly and urgently, day after day, letters, notes, journals, with a rapid and imperious pen, concerned only with making her meaning plain, her sentiments indubitable.

It is now quite impossible for anyone to write, or even to think, about Queen Victoria without an immediate glow of prejudice. To some a joke, to others an idol, she impressed or imposed herself upon the minds of her people in a way quite unknown since the days of the royal Tudors. Her influence in politics may never have been decisive, or even very considerable, yet she certainly modified, in ways not at all ambiguous, the pattern and habit of respectable society. One may indeed say that one of her first purposes was to make society respectable. Without humour, without any notable charm of manner and with little natural benevolence, always laying stress on points of privilege and upholding with a stubborn dullness the most reactionary ideas, the Queen was none the less triumphant. She floated through a phase of unpopularity into her solemn Jubilee splendours, and by 1887 she was unquestionably the most important person in her dominions.

The letters of Queen Victoria, whatever we may think of them, have thus a unique value and importance. They are also notable intrinsically on account of their style. Royalty, immune from the ordinary consequences of imprudence, may scribble with peculiar freedom. But the Queen was no scribbling maniac like George III; when she wrote she wrote with purpose and insistency. She was ready most unscrupulously to use her prerogative, not as a queen but as a woman—for example, when she requested Melbourne (in 1840) to avoid a Ministerial crisis, for "it might make her *seriously ill.*" Her interest in military affairs was very strongly marked, although her knowledge was imperfect and she was totally incapable of understanding "the common soldier." In 1854, when the tragedy of the Crimean winter was appalling the British public, her main concern was not with blankets or great coats but with medals. What was a little cold in comparison with "*glory* and honourable warfare"? (One recalls the savage irony of one of Leech's drawings in *Punch*.) Of attempts at political intervention there are many instances, as in 1863 when she tells Granville that "*we* must, on NO account, let ourselves be dragged into what *may* be a war with Germany," and in 1867 when she gave Derby her views on the subject of Reform. To her the Franco-Prussian War of 1870 was a dreadful affliction: she saw "the country she loves best next her own [Germany] . . . in peril of the gravest kind, insulted and attacked." Those who disagreed with her were "unpatriotic"; they did not see what was "necessary"; they did not hold the "*right* views." Her own sense of right was, to her, quite as obvious and as indisputable as the laws of gravity. Albert, too, had been infallible, and in her widowed years the Queen often invoked his example. Yet I wonder what Albert would have thought if he had seen her supporting the Deceased Wife's Sister Bill (in 1883) and heard her denouncing the arguments against it as "low and unworthy." Again and again the heat of indignation burns along her seething lines. The Queen is "*quite* furious at anyone daring or presuming to say *she* wanted to make war on Russia"; she is exasperated by the perky taunts of Lord Randolph Churchill and his "*marvellous* want of knowledge of history." Raging strokes of the pen— one, two or three—underline the significant word, until her letters fairly seem to hiss.

The Queen was romantically fond of Disraeli, who was always "right," and she hated Gladstone, who was always "wrong." Mr. Gladstone was

THOMAS HENRY HUXLEY, 1825-1895
Pencil drawing by A. Legros

largely concerned, in his letters, with political analyses; but the letters of Mr. Disraeli (a rare literary showman) are lively and emotional.

Disraeli was a performer who was never in any doubt concerning his powers. "I was heard with the greatest attention and good humour immediately," he wrote to his sister in 1838; again, in 1841: "I spoke with great effect last night in the House"; and yet again, in 1859, "—the grandest speech I ever made: all say so." There never was a greater master of elegant insincerity, never a man so expert in the choice of tone. When Lady Blessington died he wrote at once to D'Orsay: "I find sometimes a melancholy pleasure in recalling her cordial and accomplished existence"; and in 1863 we find him assuring the Queen that "His acquaintance with the Prince is one of the most satisfactory incidents of his life: full of refined and beautiful memories." Always a highly successful humbug, Mr. Disraeli was not mistaken when he declared (in 1873) "I owe everything to woman." Even at the age of seventy he could still write to Lady Bradford: "To love as I love, and rarely to see the being one adores . . ."

Mr. Gladstone was a zealous collector of letters—he had in his fireproof Octagon about sixty thousand, which included many angry notes from the Queen. But he was too grimly intellectual, his moral fixtures were too rigid, for the sprightlier pleasures of writing, and his own letters are reserved and austere.

37

DAVID LIVINGSTONE, 1813-1873
Pencil drawing by Joseph Bonomi, 1857

These are the two men who had the greatest effect upon Victorian political history. There are two others who had a far greater effect upon the whole course of knowledge and of speculative thought in the same period: Charles Robert Darwin and Thomas Henry Huxley. Both were admirable letter-writers. Both had a manly, humorous and energetic style, and although Huxley was the more accomplished writer of the two (he has a very definite place in literature as well as in science), he never surpassed his friend in clarity and honesty of expression. I know nothing to equal the freshness of Darwin's letters written during the voyage of the *Beagle* in 1834. He sends his love to his old nurse—"tell her, if she was now to see me with my great beard, she would think I was some worthy Solomon come to sell the trinkets." He had the modesty and the honourable nature of a great man, and when, in 1858, he was about to publish the *Origin of Species* and discovered that Wallace had independently arrived at the same conclusion, he wrote in distress to Lyell: "I would rather burn my whole

38

book, than that he or any other man should think I had behaved in a paltry spirit." A happy solution was found in the reading of a joint paper before the Linnaean Society. In the following year he wrote to Huxley: "I am . . . hydropathising and coming to life again, after having finished my accursed book, which would have been easy work to any one else, but half-killed me." Replying to a criticism by Lyell, he said: "You are right, there is a screw out here." And he was patient with earnest questioners, gently assuring Mrs. Boole, for instance, that the problem of free will and necessity "has been found by most persons insoluble."

Huxley was not so patient. He had a pugnacity of disposition which made him occasionally rough. At the age of twenty-five (in 1850) he wrote to his sister: "There are many nice people in this world for whose praise or blame I care not a whistle . . . I will leave my mark somewhere, and it shall be clear and distinct . . . and free from the abominable blur of cant, humbug and self-seeking which surrounds everything in this present world." This was a personal manifesto, and it provides the key to his life and achievement. Undeterred by the fact that a scientist might "earn praise but not pudding," he went forward with the sword of truth in his hand. And although he told Lyell in 1860 that "five-sixths of women will stop in the doll stage of evolution to be the stronghold of parsondom," he was extremely happy in his married life. Many of his letters to his family are deliciously playful and are embellished with gay little drawings. But there must have been times when his precision of utterance was almost alarming. "I love my friends and hate my enemies," he declared with unregenerate honesty. He lived in a world of solid phenomena; his ideas were innately positive. But his fine letters to Kingsley show that he respected and loved sincerity of opinion, even in those with whom he was unable to agree. It is to the credit of Kingsley that he was good friends with a man who wanted schoolmasters to be "scientific missionaries to convert the Christian Heathen of these islands to the true faith" (letter to Dohrn in 1871). Declining health in his last years did not impair the brilliance or vivacity of his letters, and it is odd that he should have described letter-writing as the *"bête noire"* of his existence.

Uncompromising honesty and equal courage of another type are to be found in the letters of David Livingstone (1813-1873), the man who trod so fearlessly in the hidden ways of darkest Africa, preaching, healing and exploring. They are strange letters. Their pious expressions often recall the style of John Wesley. He saw the Africans as "captives of sin and Satan," and yet they got on very well together. He was naturally annoyed when a Boer commando under Pretorius wrecked his home at Kolonberg during his absence (1852), but he could not help thinking with amusement of "a big fat Boeress drinking coffee out of my kettle, and then throwing her tallowy corporeity on my sofa." Although he trusted in Providence, he trusted in good guns as well, and the loss of his weapons distressed him greatly. When he visited England in 1858 he wore a black coat and blue trousers and a cap with a stripe of golden lace. He saw Newstead in 1864. "His character does not shine," he wrote in reference to Byron: "It appears to have been horrid." Yet Livingstone was no sour evangelist. He was frequently jocose. The gentleman who sent him clothes that were too big was asked if "he thought Aldermen grew in Africa"; and when he heard of people who said "Christianity made the blacks worse"—"tell that to the young trouts," he wrote. His calm and slightly cynical account of the meeting with Stanley in 1871 is in strong contrast with Mr. Stanley's abominably vulgar journalism.

The best letters are generally, though not always, written by the best writers. But the great epistolary ages are past. Long before the close of the nineteenth century it would have been impossible to find a group of letter-writers at all comparable to those of Johnson's day. That is not to say that we do not find letters of extraordinary brilliance in this later period. We certainly do: but there are fewer of them, and, in the case of literary people, they do not occupy a high place among the works of their writers.

I have dealt separately and in some detail with Queen Victoria's letters because of their position and importance. But, in a final survey of particular categories, it is proper to say something of English royal letters as a whole.

No letters are more reverently treated by their editors, none are presented with more ample comment or with greater ostentation, and yet one has to allow that most of them are among the dullest of the historian's documents. George III, for instance, wrote a tremendous number of letters, most of them displaying little except irritable stupidity and affording sad evidence of a neurotic's desire to obtain mental relief. The horrible self-abasement of the earlier letters to Bute (so clearly pathological), the twaddling pomposity of the notes angrily scribbled in the course of the American War, are not very likely to please an ordinary, sensible reader.

It is far otherwise in the case of our tremendous Tudors—Henry VIII and Queen Elizabeth. These robust and imperious royal persons wrote with energy, style and wit. Even in his official correspondence Henry delighted in vigorous assertion. His verbal armoury was immense, his erudition never contemptible. The letter to the Judges in 1535 is a famous example of his power and eloquence, and his epistle to the Bishop of Durham (1538) shows him adept in all the turns of theological argument. His love letters to Anne Boleyn, the mother of Queen Elizabeth, reveal an affection that is clearly unsimulated. "Mine own sweetheart, this shall be to advertise you of the great elengeness that I find here since your departing . . . wishing myself (especially an evening) in my sweetheart's arms, whose pretty dukkys I trust shortly to kiss." In signing these letters he sometimes used the device of combined and embracing initials: "H. (A B) R." And he would record the time and occasion: "Written after the killing of a hart, at eleven of the clock."

THE MAIL COACH.
Water colour by C. Cooper Henderson, 1803-1877
By courtesy of The Fine Art Society

QUEEN VICTORIA'S FIRST COUNCIL, JUNE 20TH, 1837
Study in water colour by Sir David Wilkie
By gracious permission of H.M. The King

There are only a small number of letters written in the hand of Queen Elizabeth. Although she inherited her father's energetic manner, she lacked his noble verbosity and reliable scholarship. In her familiar style she was fond of stilted conceits and an affectation of elegant learning not altogether warranted by endowment or knowledge. This affectation was more assertive in her later years, and a good example is the playful charter to Burghley in 1591, in which he is addressed as "the disconsolate and retired sprite, the eremite of Theobalds . . . the abandonate of Nature's fair works and Servant to Heaven's wonders." The famous note written to Dr. Cox, Bishop of Ely, in 1573 is of a very different complexion: "Proud Prelate . . . If you do not immediately comply with my request, I will unfrock you, by God." Sometimes, as in her letters to Burghley and Shrewsbury, there is a most unroyal display of tenderness, and she signs herself "Your most loving sovereign. . . Your faithful, loving Sovereign."

Our Stuart letters, in spite of adroit and enthusiastic editorial presentation, are for the greater part exceedingly dull. Some of the letters of Charles II to his sister the Duchess of Orleans ("Madame") show facility of expression, although one is not likely to be much interested in accounts of royal colics and headaches.

We cannot leave our kings, princes and governors without a reference to Cromwell. "You know," he said in 1648 to Lord Wharton, "how untoward I am at this business of writing." He wrote as he spoke, very plainly, in a harsh, concise manner, with vehement sincerity and unswerving faith in the Lord of Israel. For the friendship and the favour of men he cared but little, counting among his own allies Jehovah. His religion was of that precise and literal nature to which the terms of bigotry and enthusiasm are frequently applied, and his use of pious phrases may sometimes offend, or merely amuse, a careless reader. But there was no hypocrisy in Cromwell. It was this very faith, combined with true genius in the handling of cavalry, which made him almost invincible in the field. He was at his best when describing action, as in his letters to Lenthall after the Worcester fight (1651): "The dispute was long and very near at hand, and often at push of pike, and from one defence to another."

This manly simplicity is typical of soldiers' letters at all times. I wish I could have included in this essay many quotations from such letters, especially from those written before the age of censorship, when the soldier could, and did, send home unrestrained accounts of what was really happening.

There are many to choose from, but I can here select only two writers: Captain Bowles of the Coldstream Guards, who wrote from the Peninsula (1809-1813), and Paymaster Dixon, who wrote from the Crimea (1854-1856). The letters of the first were published in the Malmesbury Correspondence (1844); quotations from Dixon will be found in my book on the Crimean War (1939).

41

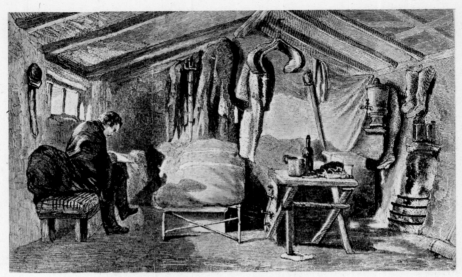

INTERIOR OF AN OFFICER'S HUT AT BALACLAVA
Woodcut by Constantin Guys, 1854

Bowles is among the best of military letter-writers; gay, observant, occasionally grim, always readable. Without any pretence of style he has a natural eye for what is telling, whether in colour or detail. He notes how the monks of Batalha in their white gowns waited upon the red-coated English officers at their table; how the troops entering Coimbra were greeted with showers of holy water and of dried rose-leaves; how the Spaniards fled from the battle of Talavera "screaming with terror." He has much to say about the amusements of the army (of the officers, at any rate) in 1811: coursing, hunting, shooting and theatricals. They had a pack of hounds which, he says, "has already knocked up the horses of the staff." They had a "tolerable show of woodcocks, partridges, snipes, hares and rabbits." Thus he writes (as Tom Burke or Charles O'Malley might have written) of the lighter side of the campaign. He writes with equal frankness of its horrors. At the storming of Ciudad Rodrigo (1812) they found some twenty English deserters in the citadel, more than one of whom was killed in defending the breach. After the bloody fall of Badajoz "nearly a dozen females were actually murdered or died of ill usage"; and at San Sebastian "every species of enormity was committed." That is what happened when towns were taken after bitter fighting. It was otherwise, we may hope, at Vittoria (1813)—"Nearly the whole of the *female* establishment of the French army was captured, which rather overstocked us with that article." The sporting tradition was observed in the Crimea, and there were even

42

sporting ladies like the dashing Mrs. Duberly, but, in the letters of Pay-master Dixon, the tragedies of that gruesome war predominate. Writing in November 1854, when our unprovided army was literally wasting away, he says that "numbers of officers have sent in their resignations." In January 1855: "We (the Royal Fusiliers) have had eleven hundred men since we left England . . . and we cannot now raise 240 to go on parade. . . . It is truly awful to see such sights—I'd rather far go over twenty fields of battle." At the end of the month: "I will stick to what I said before about the Staff, etc. Apathy, mismanagement and misrule are the prevailing qualities." And when the first anniversary of Inkerman was celebrated in 1855 (after the fall of Sevastopol) Dixon could write, "I am the sole remnant of the Regiment of that day." Such letters were reaching England in hundreds, and these, with Russell's famous dispatches in *The Times*, were largely instrumental in bringing about improvements and reforms.

To make a selection of letters written in the middle and later nineteenth century and in our own period is obviously difficult. Of course there are people like Mr. Bernard Shaw who are so highly charged with original brilliance or perverse mischief that anything they write will be worth read-ing. Indeed, it seems impossible for Mr. Shaw to take up his pen without the flash of a paradox or some notable oddity of diction, or (it may be) the crackle of preposterous and enthralling nonsense; but these tricks are not of the genuine epistolary nature; they are not so much a personal revelation as a highly spectacular grinding of axes. The letters of Wilde, also, are perhaps too deliberately brilliant. I myself am fond of the letters of George Meredith (1828-1909); I think they are personal in the true sense, and have a warmth and lucidity which are not to be found in the intricate prose of his books.

One of the finest letter-writers of the nineteenth century was unquestion-ably Edward FitzGerald (1809-1883), who, although he is now chiefly known for his plausibly mellifluous translation of Omar Khayyám, was admirable and original in his prose. He wrote in 1838 to Barton, "I like to sail before the wind over the surface of an even-rolling eloquence," and this is what he succeeded in doing, for no one has a smoother, more melodious epistolary style. Perhaps the craftsmanship is always deliberate, the phrases always polished and the periods always running to a studied cadence, and he cer-tainly repeated the same turns or felicities in letters to different people. He was invariably elegant, and it was natural that he should have protested in 1880 against the use of such words as "jolly," "beastly" and "awful." His letters are those of a pleasant, accomplished and original character, delightfully presented.

The same note of studied accomplishment is observable in the letters of Robert Louis Stevenson (1850-1894). Stevenson was a master of style, highly skilled in fashioning the bright "ring of words," and extremely

43

interested in the analysis of harmonies. But the harmonies of Stevenson are never orchestral, his thoughts are neither surprising nor profound. His letters are full of charming fancy and easy narrative; and he always wrote well, even in his earliest youth.

The letters of D. H. Lawrence (1885-1930) were portentously and religiously produced some years ago (1932) with an introduction by Mr. Aldous Huxley. Our interest in this collection will depend upon our interest in Lawrence and our estimate of his position in literature. These are matters of opinion, although we can have no doubt at all of Lawrence's tremendous powers of self-revelation and of his occasionally sublime insight. Yet there are many to whom his letters may seem to be the fretful, sickly effusions of a harried and irritable nature with a vigorous and intrusive sexual preoccupation. He himself was well aware of his tragic singularity. "I do not belong to the ship." In 1917, after he had been granted exemption from military service, he wrote "there *is not* any England." He wandered about the world in search of peace and realisation, without ever finding them. Although he was tormented always by the consuming egoism of the artist, it is impossible not to feel that the true problem of Lawrence was pathological. We can scarcely form any other opinion of the man who declares that he is engaged in "the fight for the phallic reality." His obsessions may exasperate, his "philosophy" arouse derision, yet his letters are certainly among the most remarkable of recent years, and some of them (for example, the letter to Willard Johnson about the Turquoise Horse) are exquisitely beautiful.

Another modern collection which is of intrinsic value as the record of a strange and eminently picturesque existence is *The Letters of T. E. Lawrence* (1888-1935) edited and published in 1938 by David Garnett. Again, personal delight in these letters will depend, as in the case of the other Lawrence, upon the attitude of the reader. Only extreme reverence, I fancy, could sustain anyone through a perusal of the 800 pages of letters which Mr. Garnett has printed. T. E. Lawrence combined in a singularly vigorous way the qualities of the scholar, the artist and the man of action. It is, we may be inclined to suppose, chiefly this most unusual association of qualities which made him remarkable. But perhaps we may be tempted to say of him, as he did of E. M. Forster—"Very good; but is he quite great?"

Gertrude Bell, whose letters were published in 1927, may be regarded as a minor feminine counterpart of T. E. Lawrence. Of her letters, Lawrence himself said "they are very good, and well display her eagerness and emotion . . . she had no great depth of mind." But, he added, she was "a wonderful person." One cannot imagine a juster summary. Gertrude Bell was versatile and enthusiastic, with entirely objective preoccupations. Although she got on so well among the Arabs it is doubtful whether she understood them, or, indeed, whether she was able to assess anything profound or subtle.

T. E. LAWRENCE, 1888-1935
Oil painting by Augustus John

Three other collections of modern letters must be mentioned, although briefly, on account of their great personal and literary interest: the letters of Sir Walter Raleigh (1861-1922), the *Pollock-Holmes Letters*, and the letters of J. B. Yeats and his son W. B. Yeats. These, in their different ways, are notably fine examples of modern letter-writing, possibly, in some respects, the finest examples; but they are rarities, only serving to confirm and illuminate the dictum that the great English epistolary age was over before the middle period of Queen Victoria's reign.

LETTER FROM J. B. YEATS TO LILY YEATS FROM NEW YORK, JUNE 26th, 1914
'Lily dining with the Lord Chancellor'

There are certain conventional modes which, although epistolary in style, are not in the proper sense genuine letters. The epistolary method in fiction is massively represented in this country by Richardson's novels, and in a more frivolous way by *Humphry Clinker* and various minor works. It is now customary to look upon Richardson as a bore, yet Stevenson considered that he wrote "with the pen of an angel." Of his importance in the history of the English novel, and of his power and fluency as a writer, there cannot be any doubt.

46

Letters to the papers are so varied, so infinitely entertaining, so spontaneously representative of our national life in every phase that I am sorry to be unable to discuss them here. Nor can I speak of those "open epistles," once a favourite vehicle of attacks upon our statesmen; a type which attained a classic splendour of malevolence and unwelcome truth in the case of "Junius."

But I cannot end without a word in praise of the private anonymous letter, which is often so vigorous, amusing and informative. I wish we could have an anthology of these, even if it might be undesirable to give the names of their recipients. Frantic females write the best of them, and they are always abusively sincere. Indeed, they are the only letters of whose perfect sincerity there can be no question at all. Of love letters we may have our doubts, but hate letters are above suspicion and should always be treasured. We are far too ready to denounce the people who write them, and we do so because there is nothing we dread so much as honesty. I do not say that all the anonymous or pseudonymous are worthy of our highest regard, but it would be most ungenerous to exclude them altogether from our survey of the English Letter Writers.

'HEREWITH A PICTURE OF MY CAT'
Letter from J. B. Yeats to Lily Yeats

W. B. YEATS, 1865-1939
Pencil sketches by Augustus John

SHORT BIBLIOGRAPHY

J. Boswell. *Letters*. Edited by C. B. Tinker. 2 vols. 1924

C. Brontë. *The Brontës : their lives, friendships and correspondence*. T. J. Wise and J. A. Symington. 4 vols. 1932

G. G. N. Byron, Baron Byron. *Letters and Journals*. Edited by R. E. Prothero. 6 vols. 1898-1901

P. D. Stanhope, Fourth Earl of Chesterfield. *Letters*. Edited by B. Dobrée. 6 vols. 1932

W. Cowper. *Letters*. Edited by T. Wright. 4 vols. 1904. *Unpublished and Uncollected Letters*. 1925

T. Creevey. *The Creevey Papers*. Edited by H. Maxwell. 2 vols. 1904

M. Delany. *Autobiography and Correspondence*. Edited by Lady Llanover. 6 vols. 1861-1862

E. FitzGerald. *Letters and Literary Remains* Edited by W. A. Wright. 7 vols. 1902-1903

T. H. Huxley. *Life and Letters*. By L. Huxley. 2 vols. 1900

S. Johnson, Dr. *Letters*. Edited by G. Birkbeck Hill. 1892. *Some Unpublished Letters*. Edited by J. D. Wright, 1932

J. Keats. *Letters*. Edited by M. Buxton Forman. 1935

D. H. Lawrence. *Letters*. Edited by A. Huxley. 1932

T. E. Lawrence. *Letters*. Edited by D. Garnett. 1938

Leveson Gower, Lord Granville. *Private Correspondence*. Edited by the Countess Granville. 2 vols. 1917

E. Montagu. *Letters (1720-1761)*. Edited by E. H. Climenson. 1906. *Letters (1762-1800)*. Edited by R. Blunt. 1923

Lady M. Wortley Montagu. *Letters and Works*. Edited by Lord Wharncliffe, with additions, etc. by W. M. Thomas. 2 vols. 1893

D. Osborne. *Letters to William Temple*. Edited by E. A. Parry. 1903

The Paston Letters. Edited by J. Gairdner. 3 vols. 1895

L. Sterne. *Letters*. Edited by L. P. Curtis. 1935

R. L. Stevenson. *Letters*. Edited by S. Colvin. 4 vols. 1926

J. Swift. *Correspondence*. Edited by F. E. Ball. 6 vols. 1910-1914. *Journal to Stella*. Edited by F. Ryland. 1908

H. Walpole. *Letters*. Edited by Mrs. Paget Toynbee. 16 vols. 1903-1905

J. B. Yeats. *Letters to his son, W. B. Yeats, and others*. Edited by Joseph Hone, 1944